Young Women

ACTIVITIES

Revised Edition

JENNIFER JACKSON AND **BETH LEFGREN**

DESERET
BOOK

SALT LAKE CITY, UTAH

First printing, book 1, 1997
First printing, book 2, 1999
First printing, revised and combined edition, 2009

Library of Congress Catalog Card Number: 96-79581

ISBN-10 1-57008-298-7 (book 1)
ISBN-13 978-1-57008-298-6 (book 1)
ISBN-13 978-1-57008-621-4 (book 2)
ISBN-13 978-1-60641-185-8 (revised and combined edition)

Printed in the United States of America
Malloy Lithographing Incorporated, Ann Arbor, MI

10   9   8   7   6   5   4   3   2   1

Activities

Contents

Contents

Contents

Preface

This book was written to meet the very special needs of the young women and the Young Women program. The activities suggested in this book provide unlimited opportunities to strengthen and teach these young people. They can supply a great deal of fun in a gospel-oriented atmosphere. What better way to reach each young woman than through wholesome, enjoyable activities?

Although this book was written with the Young Women program in mind, you will find the activities useful in any of the organizations in the Church, as well as in the family. We wish you well in whatever capacity you are using this book.

Using the Activities

This section contains a wide variety of activities. We have endeavored to offer a large selection to meet your needs. To assist you in the use of these activities, we offer the following suggestions:

1. The activities are designed to reinforce specific Young Women values. Notice that the activities have value references after the activity title. These references will help you determine which activities are best suited for enhancing particular lessons from the Young Women lesson manuals. (For your assistance, a value index immediately follows this overview.)

2. Discuss each activity in your youth presidency meeting. Allow your youth presidency to take an active part in planning and preparing for the activities. This is an excellent opportunity for them to develop leadership skills. Delegation of responsibilities is an important part of involving the youth in the activities.

3. Parents can be a valuable resource for your program. Inquire about parents' specific talents and use them often. This will be a great help to you and will strengthen the young women's relationships with their families.

We know that as you apply these guidelines you will experience wonderful success!

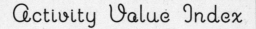

Activity Value Index

Adopt a Grandma
Divine Nature, Individual Worth, Good Works

Gospel Purpose

To develop the many qualities of charity.

Activity Description

The young women will friendship an elderly sister in the ward.

Preparation

1. Discuss the activity in your youth presidency meeting. For youth involvement, select appropriate assignments from this preparation section.
2. Prayerfully select an elderly sister in your area for your class to friendship.
3. Plan at least five occasions to show her acts of kindness. These may include giving her a special treat, doing service projects for her, giving a short musical presentation, writing letters of love and appreciation, taking pictures of her with the young women, visiting with her to learn about her early life, reading with her, and so on. Schedule these activities and delegate to involve all of the young women.

Materials Needed: Determined by chosen activities.

Activity

- Follow the prepared schedule of activities.
- Continue to friendship the sister. As a group, remember her on her birthday and other special occasions.

Halloween
Service Activity
Divine Nature, Individual
Worth, Good Works

Gospel Purpose

To learn to comfort and uplift others.

Activity Description

The young women will visit a hospital pediatric or maternity ward, giving a gift with each visit.

Preparation

1. Discuss the activity in your youth presidency meeting. For youth involvement, select appropriate assignments from this preparation section.
2. Arrange with a local hospital to have the young women deliver Halloween gifts in the maternity and/or pediatric wards. Explain the purpose of the activity. This activity is usually permissible if the group goes during visiting hours and is quiet.
3. The young women should earn money to purchase small gifts for the patients. The gifts could be coloring books, crayons, reading books, baby booties, baby wipes, fruit, etc.
4. The young women should wear appropriate costumes (nothing that would frighten the small children).
5. Provide for adequate transportation, if necessary. Fill out any travel permits required by your ward and stake.

Materials Needed: Small gifts to deliver.

Activity

- Travel to the hospital and meet at the nurses' station. Check to see if there are any rooms you should not disturb.
- As a group go quietly from room to room. Knock on each door, greet each patient, and wish him/her a happy Halloween. Leave each patient a small gift.

Evening of Traditions
Individual Worth, Knowledge, Choice and Accountability

Gospel Purpose

To provide a sharing experience between the young women and their parents.

Activity Description

Each young woman and her parent(s) will talk about and show one or two family traditions to the other young women.

Preparation

1. Discuss the activity in your youth presidency meeting. For youth involvement, select appropriate assignments from this preparation section.
2. Contact each young woman and her parent(s) to explain the purpose of this activity. Ask them to talk together and decide on one or two traditions they could share with the other young women. Help them understand that traditions can include recipes, celebration activities, songs, etc.
3. Prepare light refreshments.

Materials Needed: Contact young women for any specific needs.

Activity

- Briefly discuss the importance of family traditions and suggest some ways a tradition can be started.
- Ask one of the young women and her parent(s) to tell about their tradition.
- Repeat until everyone has had the opportunity to share a tradition or two.
- Have the young women serve the refreshments.

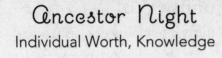

Ancestor Night
Individual Worth, Knowledge

Gospel Purpose

To understand more about an ancestor.

Activity Description

Each young woman will bring a memento or heirloom to the activity and tell other class members about an ancestor.

Preparation

1. Discuss the activity in your youth presidency meeting. For youth involvement, select appropriate assignments from this preparation section.
2. Contact each young woman and have her talk with her parents or grandparents about an ancestor. Ask her to bring something (an heirloom, a story, a recipe, etc.) associated with that ancestor.
3. If you wish, you can give each young woman a "My Ancestor" sheet, found on the following page, to assist her in finding out about her ancestor.

Activity

- Seat the young women in a circle.
- Ask one of the young women to tell the others about what she brought and what she found out about her ancestor.
- Give each girl a chance to talk about what she brought.
- When everyone has had that opportunity, ask the young women if they learned anything new about other ancestors. Encourage discussion.

My Ancestor

Full name: _____

Relationship to me (parent, grandparent, etc.): _____

Enters Mortality

When he/she was born: _____

Where he/she was born: _____

Description: _____

Parents: _____

Older brothers and sisters: _____

Grows Up

Places lived: _____

Younger brothers and sisters: _____

Schools attended: _____

Friends: _____

Hobbies, interests, awards: _____

Childhood or teenage experiences: _____

Finds a Mate

Name of spouse: _____

Marriage took place at: _____

Ceremony performed by: _____

Wedding day story: _____

Becomes a Parent

Children born (oldest to youngest): _____

Places lived: _____

Jobs held: _____

Hobbies or interests: _____

Church or civic responsibilities: _____

Leaves Mortality

Date of death: _____

Place of death: _____

Funeral information: _____

Legacy

Stories or characteristics remembered about this ancestor: _____

Facts about any heirloom, recipe, picture, etc.: _____

Gospel Purpose

To learn more about the First Presidency and the Quorum of the Twelve Apostles and prepare for general conference.

Activity Description

The young women will play games that will help them identify each member of the First Presidency and of the Quorum of the Twelve Apostles. Conference Tic-Tac-Toe should be taken home, filled out during conference, and brought back to the next activity or Sunday meeting.

Preparation

1. Discuss the activity in your youth presidency meeting. For youth involvement, select appropriate assignments from this preparation section.
2. Gather pictures of all of the members of the First Presidency and of the Quorum of the Twelve Apostles.
3. Write the name of each one of these fifteen Brethren on a wordstrip and make fifteen number squares.
4. Run off a copy of Conference Tic-Tac-Toe (page 23) for each young woman. Decide whether class members will need to complete one row (three in any direction) or fill in all of the game squares. You may also choose to limit the responses to any one conference session or allow a combination of any sessions. If you desire, give a small reward for each completed game sheet that is returned.
5. Prepare your game area by taping the pictures, in a random order, on a wall or corkboard. Place a number on each picture and the wordstrips to the side.

Materials Needed: A picture of each member of the First Presidency and of the Quorum of the Twelve Apostles, fifteen wordstrips and number squares, several copies of the previous conference *Ensign*, tape, paper, pencils.

Activity

Game: Match the Name

- Have the young women work together to identify each member of the First Presidency and of the Quorum of the Twelve Apostles and put the correct name under each picture.
- Tell the young women when a picture is identified correctly. Occasionally tell something interesting about one of the Brethren.

Game: Arrange the Order

- Have the young women work together to arrange the pictures according to the Brethren's order of seniority within the Quorum. Alternative: Place the pictures in the order of the men's ages, oldest to youngest.

Game: Find the Topic

- Divide the young women into groups and give each group a May or November Conference *Ensign*, a piece of paper, and a pencil.
- Give each group five minutes to identify the topic that each member of the First Presidency and of the Quorum of the Twelve Apostles spoke on during that conference. The group with the highest number of correct topics wins the game.

Game: Conference Tic-Tac-Toe

- Give each girl a Tic-Tac-Toe paper (page 23) to take home and use for conference.
- Briefly explain the rules you decided upon.

Conference Tic-Tac-Toe

What session did I listen to? _____	Speakers I listened to: _____ _____ _____ _____	A story I enjoyed hearing about: _____ _____ _____ _____
Scripture or scripture story used: _____ _____ _____ _____	What choir sang? _____ One of the hymns they sang was: _____ _____	Some of the topics that General Authorities spoke on were: _____ _____ _____
A speaker I enjoyed was: _____ He spoke about: _____ _____ _____	Who conducted this session? _____ Did he make any announcements? If so, what? _____ _____	After listening to conference I want to: _____ _____ _____

Arranging Flowers
Divine Nature, Individual Worth, Knowledge, Good Works

Gospel Purpose

To recognize and value others' differences.

Activity Description

The young women will learn how to make floral arrangements.

Preparation

1. Discuss the activity in your youth presidency meeting. For youth involvement, select appropriate assignments from this preparation section.
2. Make arrangements to have a specialist from a floral shop give the young women a demonstration on arranging flowers. Depending on the time of year, individual needs, and cost, you may choose to use either fresh or silk flowers. Request a variety of flower types for the demonstration.
3. Be prepared to present a short object lesson using the floral arrangement. Compare the different flowers in the arrangement to the differences in people. The variety of flowers makes a beautiful arrangement, but each flower is important. It is similar with people; everyone is important. You may discuss specific applications for your Young Women group also. See D&C 18:10.

Materials Needed: Supplies required by the florist.

Activity

- Have the demonstration on making flower arrangements.
- Give the object lesson and encourage discussion.

Follow-up Activity

- Let the girls have hands-on experience in making flower arrangements using flowers from the Young Women's garden created for the activity "Raising a Flower Garden" (p. 41). Take the arrangements to special individuals in your area.

Baking Rolls
Knowledge, Good Works

Gospel Purpose

To learn a homemaking skill.

Activity Description

Each young woman will learn to knead, shape, and bake rolls.

Preparation

1. Discuss the activity in your youth presidency meeting. For youth involvement, select appropriate assignments from this preparation section.
2. Ask someone to serve as a specialist for this activity. Be sure to explain the goals, expectations, and time constraints for this activity.

Materials Needed: Roll dough for each young woman, baking sheets, jam, butter.

Activity

- Demonstrate how to knead and shape rolls.
- Let each young woman knead and shape some roll dough.
- Leave the rolls to rise, then bake them.
- During the rising and baking time, demonstrate different ways that roll dough can be shaped or used.
- Provide butter and jam to spread on the hot rolls.
- Have the young women assist in cleanup.

Letter for the Future
Divine Nature, Choice and
Accountability, Integrity, Virtue

Gospel Purpose

To focus on setting and achieving worthwhile and eternal goals.

Activity Description

After listening to a talk on goals, each young woman will write a letter to herself. These letters will be kept for several years before they are given back to the young women.

Preparation

1. Discuss the activity in your youth presidency meeting. For youth involvement, select appropriate assignments from this preparation section.
2. Prayerfully select and invite a guest speaker. Give your speaker a topic and a specific time limit. Topic ideas could include: the value of the Young Womanhood medallion, how goals help young women understand their eternal worth, how worthy goals help young women prepare for the future, etc.
3. Determine when you will return the letters to the young women, i.e., after one year, at high school graduation, when they enter the next Young Women class, when they enter Relief Society, etc.

Materials Needed: Stationery, envelopes, pens.

Activity

- Have the young women gather to listen to the speaker.
- When the speaker has finished, give each young woman stationery, a pen, and an envelope.
- Explain to the young women that they will write a letter to themselves. Tell them when you will return these letters to them. Encourage them to describe the type of person they want to be and write about their hopes, goals, and desires.
- When they are done, have them seal their letters in the envelopes and write their names on the outsides.
- Keep the letters in a safe place until the appointed time to return them.

Lap Quilt
Knowledge, Good Works

Gospel Purpose

To show appreciation for a teacher or leader.

Activity Description

Each young woman will make a personalized quilt block for a lap quilt. During a follow-up activity, the lap quilt will be tied and given as an appreciation gift to a teacher or leader.

Preparation

1. Discuss the activity in your youth presidency meeting. For youth involvement, select appropriate assignments from this preparation section.
2. Ask someone to serve as a specialist for this activity. Be sure she understands the goals and expectations for this activity. Allow the specialist to determine the size of quilt blocks and other details.
3. Using the pattern, cut out several squares of material for the young women to use.

Materials Needed: Fabric of several different colors, washable fabric paint, straight pins, scissors, sewing machine, iron and ironing board, patterns for cutting the material squares (made from heavy cardboard or plastic canvas), yarn, fabric for the quilt back.

Activity

- Have each young woman choose nine squares of material and decide on the desired pattern of three rows of three squares.
- Let each young woman use the fabric paints or permanent markers to draw her name and a design on the center square.
- While the paint dries, have the specialist briefly talk about and demonstrate how to sew a quilt block.
- Have the young women pin and sew their quilt blocks together.

Follow-up Activity

- Show the young women how a quilt is put on a quilting frame and, if possible, allow them to assist.
- Tie the quilt and finish it.
- When it is done, have the young women present it as a gift.

Living Floral Bouquet
Individual Worth, Good Works

Gospel Purpose

To share a living gift.

Activity Description

Each young woman will plant several types of flowers in a pot. The living floral bouquets will be delivered to homebound people.

Preparation

1. Discuss the activity in your youth presidency meeting. For youth involvement, select appropriate assignments from this preparation section.
2. Purchase several types of young flowering annuals, such as petunias, alyssum, or marigolds. These should be just beginning to bud. Plan on three or four plants for each young woman.
3. Identify where the bouquets will be taken. Contact the intended recipients and inquire if live flowers will cause any problems. If so, use green plants only, and use a few silk flowers for color.
4. Ask each young woman to bring a six-inch diameter flowerpot or other deep bowl.
5. Provide for adequate transportation, if necessary. Fill out any travel permits required by the ward or stake.

Materials Needed: Gravel, potting soil, plant fertilizer, ribbon for a bow, and greeting card, if desired.

Activity

- Place about one inch of gravel at the bottom of each pot. Cover the gravel with potting soil until the pots are about half full.
- Arrange three or four different plants in each pot and fill the empty spaces with potting soil. Gently but firmly pack the soil in place.
- Following the package instructions, water and fertilize the plants.
- If desired, tie a ribbon around each pot and add a card.
- Deliver each pot to a care center or homebound individual.

Quote File
Knowledge, Choice and Accountability

Gospel Purpose

To help each young woman create a resource for talks.

Activity Description

Each young woman will find several quotes from Church magazines, write them on index cards, and begin to assemble a quote file.

Preparation

1. Discuss the activity in your youth presidency meeting. For youth involvement, select appropriate assignments from this preparation section.
2. Notify each young woman to bring two or three favorite quotes or scripture passages.

Materials Needed: Scriptures, Church magazines, index cards, pens, choice of card file boxes or rings.

Activity

- Explain what a quote is and how to decide if it would be good to have in a file.
- Give the young women several index cards and have them write their previously chosen scripture references down as their first quotes.
- Have the young women use the magazines to find quotes from General Authorities. Provide additional index cards if needed.
- If you have chosen to use the card file box, give it to the young women now. If you are using the rings, punch two holes at the top of every card and insert the rings.
- Encourage the young women to look at these quotes often and remember what they teach.

Alternate Activity

- Using a computer, show the young women how to set up their own file management system for their favorite quotes.
- Illustrate how they can use the Church Web site, http://www.lds.org, to find favorite quotes.

Follow-up Activity

- Add to their quote files by preparing your Sunday lesson quotes to fit the medium you have selected for this activity.

Scripture Picture
Faith, Choice and Accountability

Gospel Purpose

To prepare a meaningful scripture to be hung or displayed in the home.

Activity Description

Each young woman will make a framed scripture, with a pressed flower design.

Preparation

1. Discuss the activity in your youth presidency meeting. For youth involvement, select appropriate assignments from this preparation section.
2. Gather several small flowers or leaves. Place them carefully between two smooth paper towels and press them for two or three days under several heavy books. If you use a larger flower, press the petals only.
3. Before the activity, ask each young woman to decide on a favorite scripture.

Materials Needed: Heavy parchment paper, inexpensive frames with glass fronts (5" x 7" or 8" x 10"), pressed flowers, pencils, rulers, art eraser, fine-tipped permanent black markers, scissors, glue stick, toothpicks.

Activity

- Cut the parchment to fit the size of the frames.
- Have each young woman draw a pencil border about one inch from the edge of her parchment.
- Have them draw faint parallel lines inside the border and carefully write the scripture in pencil above the lines. Let them trace over the writing with the marker.
- Have the young women trace over the penciled border with the marker, using a ruler as a guide.
- Have them erase all pencil marks, after allowing the marker to dry thoroughly.
- Determine where to put the pressed flowers, and let the young women use a toothpick to place a dot of glue from the glue stick for each flower. Position the flowers.
- Disassemble the frame. Clean and thoroughly dry the glass, and place it back in the frame.
- Gently lay the parchment, scripture side to the glass, into the frame.
- Reassemble the remaining pieces of the frame.

Self-Esteem Collage
Divine Nature, Individual Worth, Virtue

Gospel Purpose

To recognize some positive personal characteristics.

Activity Description

Each young woman will make a collage that reflects her talents and interests.

Preparation

1. Discuss the activity in your youth presidency meeting. For youth involvement, select appropriate assignments from this preparation section.
2. Make a self-esteem collage as an example to show the young women.

Materials Needed: Old magazines, construction paper or poster board, glue, scissors.

Activity

- Give each young woman a piece of construction paper or poster board.
- Have them cut out pictures and words that show their interests or describe their positive traits. Let them glue the pictures onto the paper or poster board to form a collage.
- Challenge them to place the collage in a place where it will be seen every day.

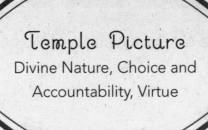

Gospel Purpose

To provide a personal reminder of the goal for temple worthiness.

Activity Description

Each young woman will assemble a wall hanging that shows a wallet-sized photo of herself and a picture of a temple.

Preparation

1. Discuss the activity in your youth presidency meeting. For youth involvement, select appropriate assignments from this preparation section.
2. Contact each young woman and have her bring a wallet-size photo of herself.
3. Make a temple picture as an example to show the young women.

Materials Needed: Inexpensive 8" x 10" frames, various colors of heavy parchment paper, rubber cement, scissors, rulers, small pictures of temples.

Activity

- Each young woman will choose two colors of parchment paper for this project. The foundation piece will measure 8" x 10" and should be a relatively neutral color. The other color will act as an accent and should complement the foundation piece.
- Have the young women measure and cut the accent-color paper $1/4$" to $1/2$" larger than their pictures.
- Let them glue the temple picture and the photo to the cut accent-color paper.
- Help the young women measure for the desired spacing on the foundation paper and glue the two pictures in place.
- Mount the parchment paper inside the frame.

Value Wreath
All Values

Gospel Purpose

To make a visual reminder of the Young Women values.

Activity Description

Each young woman will make a wreath that reflects the value colors.

Preparation

1. Discuss the activity in your youth presidency meeting. For youth involvement, select appropriate assignments from this preparation section.
2. Make a value wreath as an example to show the young women.
3. Make a heart pattern about 2 $\frac{1}{2}$ inches in diameter for each young woman.

Materials Needed: Scraps of cotton fabric in the value colors, hot-glue gun, sewing needles, white thread, pinking shears. For each young woman: 1 6-inch wooden embroidery hoop, 2" x 34" of neutral color fabric, 12" x 7" piece of bonded batting, 8 $\frac{5}{8}$-inch buttons (1 for each value color), large silk sunflower or white bow.

Activity

Each young woman will:

- Choose the fabric scraps for her value heart colors.
- Wrap the length of neutral fabric around the embroidery hoop until all of the wood is covered. Hot-glue the fabric in place.
- Using the heart pattern, cut eight hearts from the bonded batting, and two hearts from each value color.
- Sandwich the batting heart between two fabric hearts of the same color. Sew a matching colored button on top, stitching through all three layers.
- Repeat the process with each set of value color hearts.
- Arrange and hot-glue the hearts, button side out, evenly around the covered hoop.
- Hot-glue the sunflower, or white bow, at the top of the hoop. Use the tightening screw as the hanger.

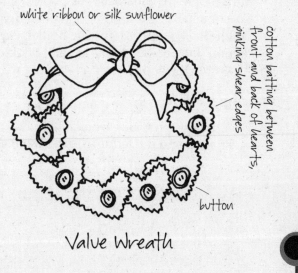

white ribbon or silk sunflower

cotton batting between front and back of hearts, pinking shear edges

button

Value Wreath

Baptism Books
Faith, Individual Worth,
Good Works

Gospel Purpose

To assist others in developing a personal understanding of the importance of baptism.

Activity Description

Each young woman will make or contribute to a simple baptism book for each of the seven-year-old children in the ward.

Preparation

1. Discuss the activity in your youth presidency meeting. For youth involvement, select appropriate assignments from this preparation section.
2. Contact the ward Primary president to get the names of the seven-year-old children. If your Primary has a standard baptism book, ask if the young women might assemble or personalize it.

Materials Needed: Copies of the *Friend* magazine, supplies necessary to decorate and assemble the book.

Activity

- Clearly explain any suggestions or guidelines the Primary president may have given. Help the young women understand the purpose of this activity.
- Ask each young woman to create a page for the books. Ideas could include using a scripture, poem, story, or simple picture. Encourage the young women to do original work for the books. However, for those that might feel uncomfortable with this, the *Friend* or other Church magazines may be used as resources.
- Make copies of each page for every book.
- To personalize each book, have each young woman write a short letter to one of the children who will receive the books, explaining their feelings about baptism and confirmation. Include one letter in each book.
- Assemble the books.

Follow-up Activity

- Encourage each young woman to attend the baptism of one of the children (preferably the one they wrote the letter to), and write a letter of congratulations to the child afterward.

Reminder Magnets
All Values

Gospel Purpose

To assist in organizing and communicating.

Activity Description

The young women will make a clothespin magnet that can hold notes, invitations, and reminders. This magnet can be used on the refrigerator, inside lockers, etc.

Preparation

1. Discuss the activity in your youth presidency meeting. For youth involvement, select appropriate assignments from this preparation section.
2. Ask the young women to wear old clothes or paint smocks for this activity.
3. Prepare the area you will be painting in; cover the floor and tabletop to prevent stains.

Materials Needed: Clothespins, self-adhesive magnetic strips, acrylic paint (or other wood paint), brushes, sponges, materials for cleanup.

Activity

- Let the young women paint the clothespins with a base coat. Let them dry.
- Have them add another coat and paint hearts, flowers, names, pin-dots, sponge designs, etc. Let that dry.
- Have the young women attach a one-inch strip of magnet to the back of the clothespin.
- Encourage the young women to use these reminder magnets to post important information about activities, goals they are working on, and so on.

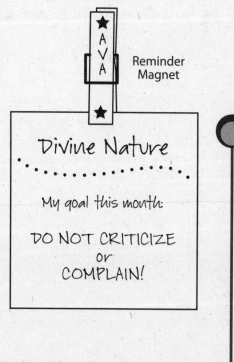

Reminder Magnet

Divine Nature

My goal this month:

DO NOT CRITICIZE
or
COMPLAIN!

Mother-Daughter Evening Out
Knowledge, Choice and Accountability, Integrity

Gospel Purpose

To encourage choosing good entertainment and to strengthen family relationships.

Activity Description

The young women will attend an uplifting cultural event with their mothers.

Preparation

1. Discuss the activity in your youth presidency meeting. For youth involvement, select appropriate assignments from this preparation section.
2. Discuss Article of Faith 13 with the young women. Stress the importance of uplifting entertainment. As a group, consider the different cultural events taking place in your area. Select a play, musical event, or dance to go to.
3. Make simple invitations for mothers or grandmothers to accompany the young women. Encourage the young women to sit by their family members at this activity.

Materials Needed: Newspapers or flyers advertising local cultural events, supplies to make simple invitations.

Activity

- Attend the cultural event as a group.
- Go to a local restaurant afterward and have a simple refreshment, such as ice cream.

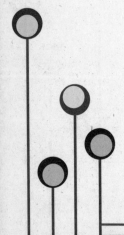

Mother-Daughter Softball

Divine Nature, Individual Worth,
Choice and Accountability

Gospel Purpose

To strengthen mother-daughter relationships.

Activity Description

The young women and their mothers will play softball together (a different sporting activity can be substituted). Refreshments will conclude the activity.

Preparation

1. Discuss the activity in your youth presidency meeting. For youth involvement, select appropriate assignments from this preparation section.
2. Discuss this activity with the young women. Explain the importance of their spending time with their mothers. Also talk about good sportsmanship.
3. Plan and prepare refreshments.

Materials Needed: Softball equipment, refreshments.

Activity

- Play softball.
- Enjoy visiting while having the refreshments.

Parent Appreciation Night
Divine Nature, Good Works, Integrity

Gospel Purpose

To express love and appreciation to parents.

Activity Description

The young women will prepare and serve a dinner for their parents. A short musical program will be presented following the meal.

Preparation

1. Discuss the activity in your youth presidency meeting. For youth involvement, select appropriate assignments from this preparation section.
2. Prepare invitations for the young women's parents.
3. Decide on a simple menu. Keep in mind that the young women should be preparing the food as much as possible.
4. Decide on table decorations.
5. Select two or three songs for the young women to present as part of a musical program following the meal. Make arrangements for an accompanist. Also schedule practice times for the young women to learn the songs.
6. Ask each young woman to write a sincere letter of love and appreciation to her parents. Seal the letter in an envelope and write the parents' names on the front. Place the letters at the table settings as name cards for seating.
7. Make assignments for the young women to conduct and give opening and closing prayers.

Materials Needed: Ingredients to prepare the meal, decorations, invitations, sheet music, writing paper, pens or pencils, envelopes.

Activity

- Welcome the parents and have an opening prayer.
- Have a young woman give a brief explanation of the parent letters.
- Serve dinner.
- Present the musical program.
- Have the closing prayer.
- Have the young women help with cleanup.

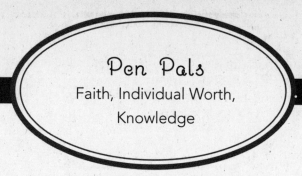

Pen Pals
Faith, Individual Worth, Knowledge

Gospel Purpose

To learn about and strengthen members of the Church in other areas.

Activity Description

The young women will write a letter to a pen pal from another area.

Preparation

1. Discuss the activity in your youth presidency meeting. For youth involvement, select appropriate assignments from this preparation section.
2. With the help of a Young Women leader from another area, obtain the names and addresses or e-mail addresses of young women that your group will be pen pals with. You will need a pen pal for each member of your Young Women group.
3. Ask each young woman to bring a small picture of herself to the activity.

Materials Needed: Stationery, envelopes, pens.

Activity

- Give each young woman the name and address of her new pen pal.
- Let them write letters. Encourage the girls to share information and ask questions about culture and beliefs.
- Read the letters together. Make sure the young women have enclosed their addresses, pictures and letters in the envelopes.
- Have them mail the letters. Give the young women mailing instructions for letters that will be sent out of the country.
- Encourage the young women to continue the correspondence with their pen pals. Ask them to share their responses with your group.

Alternate Activity

- Get permission from each young woman's parents so she can use the computer for the activity.
- Give each young woman the name and e-mail address of her new pen pal.
- Have the young women write letters to their new pen pals and e-mail their letters to them.
- Help the young women scan in their photos to send with their e-mails.
- Encourage the young women to continue the correspondence with their pen pals. Ask them to share their responses with your group.

Gospel Purpose

To support the missionary effort and strengthen testimonies.

Activity Description

Each young woman will prepare a Book of Mormon for missionary work by marking favorite scriptures and writing a brief testimony inside. The Book of Mormon will then be given to missionaries to use.

Preparation

1. Discuss the activity in your youth presidency meeting. For youth involvement, select appropriate assignments from this preparation section.
2. Ask each young woman to find several meaningful scriptures in the Book of Mormon.
3. Have every young woman bring a picture of herself (optional).
4. Obtain enough copies of the Book of Mormon for your group.

Materials Needed: Copies of the Book of Mormon, paper, red scripture pencils, pens, markers, tape or glue.

Activity

- Give each young woman a Book of Mormon.
- Ask them to mark favorite scriptures with a red scripture pencil.
- Glue or tape each young woman's picture on the inside front cover of her Book of Mormon and have her write her testimony just below it.
- Give the books to the local missionaries, or send them to a ward missionary.

Raising a Flower Garden
Faith, Knowledge, Good Works

Gospel Purpose

To teach the young women how to gain and nurture a testimony.

Activity Description

The young women will plant and raise a flower garden.

Preparation

1. Discuss the activity in your youth presidency meeting. For youth involvement, select appropriate assignments from this preparation section.
2. Select the location of your flower garden.
3. Make a work schedule for each of the young women. Assign each person regular opportunities to water, weed, and care for the flower garden.
4. Determine the types of flowers you will plant.
5. Prepare a short lesson on gaining and nurturing a testimony. Compare that process to planting seeds and growing flowers. Discuss planting, watering, and weeding. What would happen if these things were neglected in the flower garden? Liken planting to desiring a testimony, watering to reading scriptures and praying, and weeding to obedience and repentance. See Alma 32:28–30.

Materials Needed: Gardening tools, seeds.

Activity

- Present the lesson on developing a testimony.
- Let the young women help prepare the ground and plant the seeds.
- Give each young woman a schedule for caring for the garden.
- Care for the flower garden as outlined on your work schedule. Make sure a leader is always present. Find teaching moments to illustrate similarities to nurturing a testimony. What happens if the garden is not watered or weeded? What happens if our testimonies are neglected?

Follow-up Activity

- "Arranging Flowers" on page 24 is an excellent follow-up activity.
- As the plants from your garden flower, make floral arrangements to take to the elderly, those with illnesses, those in nursing homes, or to show appreciation to a leader, and so on.

Reusable Goal Chart
All Values

Gospel Purpose

To assist in setting and achieving goals.

Activity Description

The young women will make a reusable goal chart.

Preparation

1. Discuss the activity in your youth presidency meeting. For youth involvement, select appropriate assignments from this preparation section.
2. Make arrangements to laminate the goal charts.

Materials Needed: Colored paper, pencils, erasers, markers, rulers, border decorations (stickers, confetti, etc.), transparency markers.

Activity

- Let each young woman select a piece of colored paper. Give everyone a ruler, pencil, and eraser. Instruct them to use the ruler and pencil to measure in one inch from the corners of the paper. This will determine the border.

- Have the young women use the edge of the ruler as a guide to connect the measured corners with a straight line. Have them carefully trace or mark over the penciled border with a marker. This finishes the border.

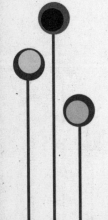

- Instruct the young women to use the pencil and ruler to mark four horizontal lines, of equal distance apart, inside the border.

- Have them use the pencil and ruler to mark six vertical lines, of equal distance apart, inside the border. This should form a grid similar to a calendar. Let the young women trace over all lines with a marker.

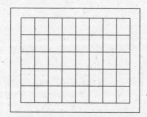

- Have the young women decorate the bottom and two side borders as desired. Leave the top border empty.
- Laminate the chart.
- Each young woman can use a transparency marker to write her goal on the top border. She can mark off a square for each day she has successfully accomplished that goal. When she has completed the chart, it can be wiped off with a damp cloth and reused. This is an excellent way to help with personal progress goals.

Follow-up Activity

- See "Reminder Magnets," page 35. These magnets can be used to hang a goal chart on the refrigerator, inside a locker, and other places.

Scripture File
Faith, Knowledge, Virtue

Gospel Purpose

To value the scriptures and apply them to life.

Activity Description

The young women will begin a scripture reference file using recipe boxes, tab dividers, and index cards.

Preparation

1. Discuss the activity in your youth presidency meeting. For youth involvement, select appropriate assignments from this preparation section.
2. Ask each young woman to bring a recipe file box and her scriptures to this activity.

Materials Needed: Alphabetical tab dividers, index cards, pens.

Activity

- Give the group four subjects to look up in the topical guides of their scriptures (Example: love, forgiveness, faith, and joy). Instruct them to read the references listed under each subject. Assist them as needed.
- They should then select one verse about each subject that is the most meaningful to them and write it on an index card.
- Teach them how to file these scripture references alphabetically, according to the first letter of the topic.

Alternate Activity

- Teach the young women how to establish an electronic file system on their computer where they can store their scripture references.
- Show the young women how to use http://www.lds.org to find their favorite scriptures.

Follow-up Activity

- Provide extra cards for scripture references that may be used in future lessons, and encourage the young women to add important scriptures to their reference files.

Service Car Wash
Good Works

Gospel Purpose

To experience the feelings of joy and satisfaction that come from service.

Activity Description

The young women will offer service to the ward members by having a free car wash.

Preparation

1. Discuss the activity in your youth presidency meeting. For youth involvement, select appropriate assignments from this preparation section.
2. Determine a date and location for the car wash. Make sure your location has adequate space to keep the vacuums and electrical cords away from the water.
3. Arrange for announcements and flyers to inform ward members of the event.
4. Encourage the young women to dress modestly and to use sunscreen and hats for protection from the sun.

Materials Needed: Hoses, buckets, cleaning solution, sponges, old towels, vacuums, extension cords.

Activity

- Divide into small task groups: washing inside windows, dashboard, etc; vacuuming interior; washing outside of vehicle; and drying vehicle.
- Rotate groups to give everyone equal opportunities.

Serving in the Library
Knowledge, Good Works, Integrity

Gospel Purpose

To provide service to the community.

Activity Description

The young women will spend time in the library assisting with erasing marks in books, restocking, dusting, repairing books, or giving any other assistance needed by the librarian.

Preparation

1. Discuss the activity in your youth presidency meeting. For youth involvement, select appropriate assignments from this preparation section.
2. Contact a local library and explain the purpose of this service project. Set up a time and date for this service.
3. Provide for adequate transportation, if necessary. Fill out any travel permits required by your ward or stake.

Activity

- Gather for appropriate opening exercises.
- Travel to the library and assist as necessary.

Sharing Ideas on Personal Worth
Divine Nature, Individual Worth, Integrity, Virtue

Gospel Purpose

To help another person realize her personal worth.

Activity Description

Each young woman will write something positive about every other member of her class. In a follow-up activity, each young woman will receive a copy of what her classmates wrote about her.

Preparation

1. Discuss the activity in your youth presidency meeting. For youth involvement, select appropriate assignments from this preparation section.
2. Ask the young women to be thinking of positive characteristics about the other members of the class.
3. Prepare a paper with the name of every class member. Make a copy for every young woman.
4. Write a special note to each young woman, commenting on her strengths, talents, and personal worth to you.
5. Contact a guest speaker for the follow-up activity. Have her speak on personal worth or another appropriate topic.

Materials Needed: Pencils, papers with each young woman's name.

Activity

- Explain the purpose of this activity, and answer any questions that may arise.
- Give each young woman a prepared paper and a pencil.
- Provide enough quiet time so that everyone will finish.
- Gather the papers.
- Pass out your personal notes as they leave.
- During the following week, compile each young woman's positive characteristics on her own personal sheet. This will make it possible for her to put her own list into her journal for future reference.

Follow-up Activity

- Gather the young women and have appropriate opening exercises.
- Listen to the guest speaker. Remind the young women that you have a special paper for each of them. Help them understand that these items are personal and do not need to be shared with other members of the class.
- Have light refreshments.
- Give each young woman her personal characteristic sheet before she goes home.

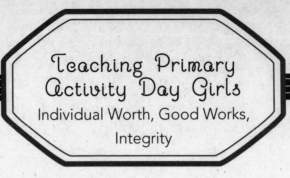

Teaching Primary
Activity Day Girls
Individual Worth, Good Works,
Integrity

Gospel Purpose

To provide meaningful service to the younger girls in the ward.

Activity Description

The young women will provide a learning activity for the Primary Activity Day girls. This activity is based on a babysitting workshop, but can be easily adapted to other ideas.

Preparation

1. Discuss the activity in your youth presidency meeting. For youth involvement, select appropriate assignments from this preparation section.
2. Contact the Activity Day leader and explain the purpose of this activity. Ask for suggestions, and coordinate schedules. The Activity Day leader may have specific goals that need to be accomplished. Be aware of these when planning the activity.
3. Contact each young woman with an assignment in teaching or assisting with the mini-classes.

Materials Needed: Materials for babysitting kits, suitable handouts for safety and first aid, light refreshments.

Activity

- Gather for appropriate opening exercises.
- Talk about babysitting safety. After a brief discussion, use role-playing to reinforce safety ideas.
- Make a simple babysitting kit. If you need ideas for this kit, go to a college (specifically, a department of early childhood development) or local extension service.
- Discuss and demonstrate basic first aid. After the demonstration, have a hands-on learning experience for the Activity Day girls.
- Conclude with light refreshments.

Treats with a Twist
Divine Nature, Individual Worth, Good Works

Gospel Purpose

To show kindness.

Activity Description

The young women will dress up in costumes and take treats to special people in the ward. This activity is especially fun in the summer—everyone is surprised!

Preparation

1. Discuss the activity in your youth presidency meeting. For youth involvement, select appropriate assignments from this preparation section.
2. Select the individuals you will visit.
3. Determine the types of treats you will be giving. Assign each of the young women to bring a specific amount. Plan enough treats to provide a light refreshment following the activity.
4. The young women should be prepared to dress up in appropriate costumes (nothing that would frighten small children).
5. Provide for adequate transportation, if necessary. Fill out any travel permits required by the ward or stake.

Materials Needed: Treats.

Activity

- Travel as a group to selected homes. Ring the doorbell and say, "Trick or Treat," and give the individuals the treat.
- Go back to the meetinghouse and enjoy refreshments.

Vegetable Garden
Faith, Knowledge, Good Works

Gospel Purpose

To give opportunities for service through work and sharing.

Activity Description

The young women will plant and care for a vegetable garden. They will also share the produce by making vegetable baskets for others.

Preparation

1. Discuss the activity in your youth presidency meeting. For youth involvement, select appropriate assignments from this preparation section.
2. Plan your basic garden layout. Select vegetables that are easy to grow in your area.
3. Organize a schedule for regular follow-up care.

Materials Needed: Gardening tools, seeds, water.

Activity

- Plant the garden as a group.
- Give follow-up care as scheduled.
- Harvest the vegetables. Prepare vegetable baskets to be given to the elderly and others with special needs in your area. On small cards write, "Wherefore by their fruits ye shall know them. —Matthew 7:20." Tuck the cards into the baskets and deliver them.

Gospel Purpose

To encourage family history work.

Activity Description

The young women will tour a local family history center (or the stake family history center), and learn about the resources available there.

Preparation

1. Discuss the activity in your youth presidency meeting. For youth involvement, select appropriate assignments from this preparation section.
2. Contact the family history center and arrange for a tour. Ask if the young women need to bring anything.
3. Assign the young women to bring any items requested by the family history center.
4. Provide for adequate transportation, if necessary. Fill out any travel permits required by your ward or stake.

Materials Needed: Pedigree charts.

Activity

- Gather for appropriate opening exercises.
- Travel to the family history center and assist the young women as necessary.
- Encourage the young women to complete a pedigree chart for their families.

Alternate Activity

- Meet with your ward family history consultants and have them show the young women how to use http://new.familysearch.org to do their family history.
- Show the young women how to use and set up on their computer a family history program, such as Personal Ancestral File (PAF), Legacy, or Family Tree Maker.

Gospel Purpose

To learn about a consumer's responsibility.

Activity Description

The young women will visit a radio (or television) station to find out how music is chosen and what impact a consumer has on those choices.

Preparation

1. Discuss the activity in your youth presidency meeting. For youth involvement, select appropriate assignments from this preparation section.
2. Make arrangements with the radio station to tour their facilities. Be sure to acquaint them with your goal.
3. Contact the young women and have them think about questions to ask during the tour.
4. Provide for adequate transportation, if necessary. Fill out any travel permits required by your ward and stake.

Activity

- Gather for appropriate opening exercises.
- Travel to the radio station and assist as necessary.

My Scripture Journal

Date: _____   Scriptural reference: _____

Who was the prophet or individual that originally wrote this scripture, or who is it about? _____

_____

What is the purpose of this scripture? What gospel principle does it teach? _____

_____

How can this scripture help me learn more about Heavenly Father and Jesus Christ?_____

_____

How do I feel about this scripture? _____

_____

☆☆☆☆☆

Date: _____   Scriptural reference: _____

Who was the prophet or individual that originally wrote this scripture, or who is it about? _____

_____

What is the purpose of this scripture? What gospel principle does it teach? _____

_____

How can this scripture help me learn more about Heavenly Father and Jesus Christ?_____

_____

How do I feel about this scripture? _____

_____

☆☆☆☆☆

Date: _____   Scriptural reference: _____

Who was the prophet or individual that originally wrote this scripture, or who is it about? _____

_____

What is the purpose of this scripture? What gospel principle does it teach? _____

_____

How can this scripture help me learn more about Heavenly Father and Jesus Christ?_____

_____

How do I feel about this scripture? _____

_____

Bishopric Dinner
Individual Worth, Knowledge, Good Works

Gospel Purpose

To learn to value and show appreciation for the bishop and his counselors.

Activity Description

The young women will prepare and serve a dinner for the bishopric and their wives.

Preparation

1. Discuss the activity in your youth presidency meeting. For youth involvement, select appropriate assignments from this preparation section.
2. Schedule a date, time, and location that will meet the needs of the bishopric.
3. If any of your bishopric have young children, either invite the children to the dinner or make appropriate babysitting arrangements.
4. Determine a simple menu that the young women can prepare.
5. Prepare tableware and decorations.
6. Assign each young woman to write a letter of appreciation to the bishop and each of his counselors.

Materials Needed: Ingredients to prepare the planned menu, tableware, decorations.

Activity

- Discuss the menu with the young women and delegate assignments for meal preparation.
- Prepare tables and decorations.
- Welcome the bishopric.
- Serve the meal.
- Present the members of the bishopric with the letters and express appreciation for all they do.
- Clean up.

Christmas Tree
Decorating
Choice and Accountability,
Good Works

Gospel Purpose

To provide a time of service and creativity.

Activity Description

The young women will decorate the ward or branch Christmas tree. This activity can also focus on decorating a tree for a needy family.

Preparation

1. Discuss the activity in your youth presidency meeting. For youth involvement, select appropriate assignments from this preparation section.
2. Contact the bishop for permission necessary for this activity.
3. Use items from "Origami" (page 64) or "Cinnamon Cutouts" (page 100); or use any other simple Christmas tree decorations.
4. Contact the young women and have them think of one of their favorite Christmas traditions.

Materials Needed: light refreshments (optional)

Activity

-   Gather the young women.
-   Give specific assignments. Be sure every young woman has an assignment that will help her feel part of the activity.
-   After the tree is decorated, serve refreshments and share family Christmas traditions.

Gospel Purpose

To encourage young women to attend temple dedications and to prepare to attend the temple.

Activity Description

The young women will make a temple handkerchief to use for temple dedications and for when they will attend the temple.

Preparation

1. Discuss the activity in your youth presidency meeting. For youth involvement, select appropriate assignments from this preparation section.
2. Depending on the size of your group, you may need to arrange for an assistant.

Materials Needed: A small, plain white handkerchief for each girl, gathered lace, white thread, straight pins, scissors, two sewing machines, acid-free envelopes (found in most large copy centers).

Activity

- Each young woman will pin lace around the edges of the handkerchief, making small tucks at the corners so the lace will lay flat.
- Stitch the lace onto the handerchief by using a zigzag stitch.
- Carefully fold the handkerchief and store it in an acid-free envelope to prevent the fabric from yellowing.

Follow-up Activity

- Plan a group trip to a nearby temple. Tour the grounds and take a picture of each young woman in front of the temple. Give them the picture to keep as an encouragement to prepare to attend the temple one day.

Job Applications
Knowledge, Choice and Accountability

Gospel Purpose

To prepare for career development.

Activity Description

Each young woman will learn about job applications and have personal help in preparing one.

Preparation

1. Discuss the activity in your youth presidency meeting. For youth involvement, select appropriate assignments from this preparation section.
2. Invite a specialist to supervise this activity. Be sure to give your specialist all the information (goals, time limits, and financial guidelines) necessary for this activity. Your ward employment specialist is a good resource.
3. Get a job application sheet from a local job service or employment agency and make enough copies for each young woman. Set up your instruction area with tables and chairs.

Activity

- Explain how to fill out the job application page correctly. Talk about the importance of filling the form completely, correctly, and neatly.
- Assist the young women in filling out their personal job applications. Answer questions as necessary.
- After the applications have been finished, briefly talk about other preparations for a job interview. Include ideas such as being on time, maintaining eye contact, dressing appropriately, knowing about the company, having a positive attitude, and so forth.

Job Interviews
Knowledge,
Choice and Accountability

Gospel Purpose

To prepare for career development.

Activity Description

Each young woman will have the opportunity to experience a preparatory job interview and learn about telephone skills. Use this activity as a follow-up for Preparing a Job Application, page 73.

Preparation

1. Discuss the activity in your youth presidency meeting. For youth involvement, select appropriate assignments from this preparation section.
2. Invite two specialists to teach the young women about basic interviewing skills and telephone manners. Encourage the use of case studies and role playing to reinforce ideas and skills. Be sure to give your specialists all the information (goals, time limits, and financial guidelines) necessary for this activity.
3. Ask several adults to assist with the job interviews.
4. Contact the young women and have them bring completed resumes. Remind them to dress appropriately for the interviews.
5. Set up the interviewing areas by providing each interviewer with a table and two chairs.

Activity

- Gather the young women together and learn about basic interviewing skills. Allow for a brief question and answer period.
- Divide the young women into two groups.
- Direct one group to the telephone manners class and the other group to the interviewing area.
- Encourage the young women to be interviewed as many times as they can in the time allotted.
- At the end of twenty to twenty-five minutes, change groups. Adjust class time depending on ages and needs.

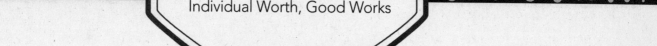
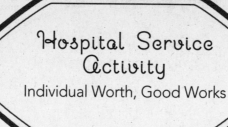

Hospital Service Activity
Individual Worth, Good Works

Gospel Purpose

To provide an opportunity for service to others.

Activity Description

The young women will deliver a small item that can be used to decorate a hospital tray.

Preparation

1. Discuss the activity in your youth presidency meeting. For youth involvement, select appropriate assignments from this preparation section.
2. Contact the hospital's public relations department for information and approval regarding this activity.
3. Use a previously made item that was completed beforehand specifically for this activity. You may want to use something from the "Origami" activity (page 64).
4. Provide for adequate transportation if necessary. Fill out any travel permits required by your ward or stake.

Materials Needed: Small note cards, envelopes, pens.

Activity

- Gather the young women.
- Give each young woman a note card and have her write a brief note of encouragement.
- Place an envelope with each tray decoration and deliver to the hospital.

Gospel Purpose

To set goals that will prepare young women for temple marriage.

Activity Description

After listening to a talk on temple marriage, each young woman will write a letter to her future eternal companion. The young women will keep the letters in a safe place until they are married.

Preparation

1. Discuss the activity in your youth presidency meeting. For youth involvement, select appropriate assignments from this preparation section.
2. Prayerfully select a couple who has been sealed in the temple to speak to your group. Ask one to speak about the preparing to go to the temple, and the other about the blessings of temple attendance.

Materials Needed: Stationery, envelopes, pens.

Activity

• Have the young women gather to listen to the speakers.
• Following the speakers, briefly discuss with the young women the necessity of preparing now to be an eternal companion. Point out that if we do not have the opportunity in this earth life to be married, it will be given to us in the next life, so all of us must prepare for this experience.
• Give each young woman stationery, an envelope, and a pen.
• Explain to the young women that they are to write a letter to their future eternal companions. Encourage them to express the things that they have committed to do to be prepared to go to the temple to be married. Also have them describe what they are doing to prepare to be good wives and mothers.
• When they are finished, have them seal the letter in an envelope and keep it in a safe place until the appointed time.

Learning to Give a Talk
Individual Worth, Knowledge

Gospel Purpose

To develop and strengthen skills necessary for organizing and presenting talks.

Activity Description

The young women will learn about a basic method of developing a talk and will, as a three person group, present a five-minute talk.

Preparation

1. Discuss the activity in your youth presidency meeting. For youth involvement, select appropriate assignments from this preparation section.
2. Write simple topics on slips of paper and place them in an empty bottle or "topic jar." Choose topics from *For the Strength of Youth* or *True to the Faith*.
3. Call a specialist. Be sure to give your specialist all the information (goals, time limits, and financial guidelines) necessary for this activity.
4. Be sensitive to the individual needs and abilities of each young woman.

Materials Needed: Scriptures, reference books, paper, pencils.

Activity

- Talk about the three main parts of a talk: introduction, body, and conclusion. Give brief examples of each.
- Tell the young women that each group will work together to prepare and give a talk on the topic they choose. Explain that each person must present a section of the talk.
- Divide the young women into groups of three. Allow each group to choose from the topic jar.
- Give the young women about fifteen to twenty minutes to prepare the talks.
- Have each group present its talk.

Becoming a Better Consumer
Knowledge, Choice and Accountability

Gospel Purpose

To become a wise user of personal resources.

Activity Description

The young women will participate separately, in pairs, or as a group in gathering consumer information about a cell phone, television, or other major product.

Preparation

1. Discuss the activity in your youth presidency meeting. For youth involvement, select appropriate assignments from this preparation section.
2. Decide which item the young women will be gathering information on. Suggest a television, computer, cell phone, or digital camera.
3. Determine what store will work best for this activity. Consider a place that has more than three brands of the product you will be pricing. When you have decided, call the manager and make any arrangements necessary to accommodate the young women's group.
4. Copy the "Comparison Buying Chart" (page 79) for each young woman.
5. Provide for adequate transportation, if necessary. Fill out any travel permits required by your ward and stake.

Materials Needed: Pencils.

Activity

- Give each young woman a "Comparison Buying Chart" and explain what information is needed to fill out the chart. Help them understand what the phrase "comparative shopping" means.
- Travel to the store. Help the young women as necessary.
- Return to the meeting house and briefly talk about the choices that were offered and how to determine the "best buy."

Comparison Buying Chart

Brand	Price	Warranty	Service Availability (Parts & Labor)		Other Information

Directing Music
Knowledge, Good Works

Gospel Purpose

To help the young women understand that as they learn and develop skills they can better serve others.

Activity Description

The young women will be taught basic patterns for leading music and given an opportunity to use this skill.

Preparation

1. Discuss the activity in your youth presidency meeting. For youth involvement, select appropriate assignments from this preparation section.
2. Select a specialist for this activity. Be sure to give your specialist all the information (goal, time limits, and so on) necessary for this activity.
3. Determine future opportunities to allow the girls to take turns leading music. (For example, in opening exercises for Sunday, opening exercises for activity nights, for songs that enrich Sunday lessons, for New Beginnings, Young Women in Excellence, and so on.)

Materials Needed: As requested by specialist.

Activity

- Introduce your specialist. Participate in learning the basics of leading music.
- Briefly discuss the value of learning new skills to benefit others. How does music help others? By learning to lead music a young woman is able to help uplift others through music.
- Make assignments for upcoming opportunities for the young women to take turns leading the music.

Follow-up Activity

- Be consistent in allowing the young women regular and frequent opportunities to practice the skill of leading music. Allow one or more young women to share this value experience at Young Women in Excellence. They can demonstrate their accomplishment through leading one of the musical selections.

Paper Flowers
Individual Worth, Good Works

Gospel Purpose

To provide an inexpensive gift for a service project. Use this activity to furnish a time for socializing, friendshipping, and building feelings of self-worth.

Activity Description

The young women will make a bouquet of paper flowers for a service project. Use this as a preparation activity before "Compassionate Service Activity" (page 96) or other service activities.

Preparation

1. Discuss the activity in your youth presidency meeting. For youth involvement, select appropriate assignments from this preparation section.
2. Cut the light pink paper into two-inch squares, the pink paper into 2.5-inch squares, the dark pink paper into three-inch squares, the red paper into 3.5-inch squares, and the green tissue into 4.5-inch squares. Use other colors if you wish to add variety to the bouquet.

Materials Needed: 5/8-inch buttons, light pink paper, pink paper, dark pink paper, red paper, green chenille stems (pipe cleaners), green tissue paper, scissors or pinking shears, all-purpose glue, glue stick.

Activity

- Give each young woman one square of each color of paper, one tissue square, a chenille stem, and one button.
- Insert the chenille stem through the bottom of the button until about two inches is on top. Bend it in half and carefully guide the other end of the stem down through another hole. Gently pull the button up to the chenille stem's bend, and then twist the stem until the button is secure.
- Have the young women take the largest paper square and fold it into a triangle.

- Fold the paper in half two more times. Always keep the shape like a triangle.

- Holding the folded corner at the bottom, round the edges with scissors. For a fancier edge use pinking shears. Cut a very small tip from the bottom of your "ice cream cone."

- Unfold and gently flatten.

- Repeat until each of the pink or red papers has been cut the same way.
- Fold the green tissue the same way but cut a deep scoop at the top of the triangle.

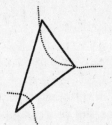 

- Glue the papers together, with the tissue on the bottom and the light pink paper on the top. Be careful to align the center holes and stagger the petal loops.
- Place a drop of all-purpose glue on the bottom of the button. Guide the chenille stem down through the center holes. Place the flower button side down, and gently press the petals onto the button.
- Let stand, upside down, until dry.
- Assemble all the flowers and arrange in a vase.

Gospel Purpose

To encourage the young women to keep a personal history.

Activity Description

The young women will take turns sharing personal experiences. Following the discussion they will record a story to begin their own personal history.

Preparation

1. Discuss the activity in your youth presidency meeting. For youth involvement, select appropriate assignments from this preparation section.
2. Ask the young women to be prepared to share two stories at the upcoming activity. The following ideas are suggestions for personal experience topics: a holiday memory, first memory of school, a job experience, a favorite vacation, a baby-sitting memory, and so on.
3. Ask each young woman to bring a binder.
4. Prepare simple refreshments.

Materials Needed: Paper, pens, sheet protectors.

Activity

- Sit in a circle or around a large table. Share refreshments as the young women take turns telling their experiences.
- Briefly discuss how enjoyable it is to hear stories about other individuals' experiences in life. It helps us to get to know them better and to learn from them. Use this to illustrate the importance of personal history.
- Pass out the paper, pens, and sheet protectors. Have the young women each write one of the stories they shared with the group. Assist as needed. Put the paper in a sheet protector and store it in the binder.
- Explain that this is the start of their personal histories. Challenge the young women to write one additional story each week and add it to their binders. Tell them to put it in an approximate chronological order. Brainstorm topics that they could write about: birthdays, pets, embarrassing moments, sporting activities, and so on.

Follow-up Activity

- If the young women have faithfully added to their personal history this binder could be displayed at Young Women in Excellence.

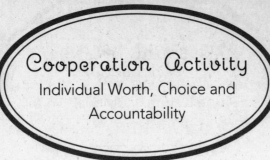

Gospel Purpose

To demonstrate the importance of cooperation in achieving goals.

Activity Description

The young women will participate in activities that teach aspects of cooperation.

Preparation

1. Discuss the activity in your youth presidency meeting. For youth involvement, select appropriate assignments from this preparation section.
2. Choose three of the cooperation activities described below or use any others that fill the purpose of this activity. Be sensitive to the needs and abilities of the young women when selecting activities.
3. Delegate responsibility for each game to an adult or specialist. Give specific information such as purpose, time limits, expected attendance, and so forth.

Materials Needed: Check selected cooperation activities to determine necessary materials.

Activity

- Briefly discuss what cooperation is and how it is important in everyday living.

Back-to-back race—Mark a course of about thirty yards. Divide everyone into trios and have each group link their elbows together to form a small circle. The young women in each group must work together to get to the finish line first.

Feather race—Mark a course of about thirty feet. Divide the young women into pairs and give each pair one feather. Using only their breath, each pair must blow its feather into the air and keep it there until they have moved it over the finish line.

Mirror Race—Mark a course of about thirty yards. Divide your group into pairs facing each other and give each pair a small, handheld mirror. Person One, who is facing away from the finish line, places her hands on her partner's shoulders. Her partner, Person Two, is facing the finish line and holding the mirror. The mirror should be held so that Person One can see the course behind her. Each pair of young women can use only the mirror to guide them to the finish line. Repeat until every person has the chance to cross the finish line.

Three-legged walk—Mark a course of about thirty yards. Pair off the young women. Tie one person's right leg to her partner's left leg. Have each team try to walk as rapidly as possible to the finish line.

Beach ball handoff—Blindfold half of the young women and have them stand in a line. Place the remaining young women on either side of the line. Explain that the object of the game is for the blindfolded girls to pass the beach ball to the person behind them, beginning at the front of the line and continuing until the last blindfolded girl in line is holding the ball. The young women who are not blindfolded will stand on either side of the line and coach the blindfolded girls as they attempt to pass the ball.

- After each game briefly discuss how cooperation was used during the game.

Gospel Purpose

Learning to use inexpensive but creative resources to prepare gifts.

Activity Description

The young women will learn about inexpensive ways to wrap gifts for their friends or family. They will also learn a simple wrapping technique.

Preparation

1. Discuss the activity in your youth presidency meeting. For youth involvement, select appropariate assignments from this preparation section.
2. Select a specialist for this activity. Be sure to give your specialist all the information (goals, time limits, and financial guidelines) necessary for this activity.

Materials Needed: Basic wrapping paper, small boxes, tape, ribbon, scissors, other materials requested by the specialist.

Activity

- Gather the young women and have the specialist talk about creative wrappings. Use ideas listed below or others that the specialist may choose.
    1. Decorate a plain brown paper bag. Use markers, stickers, craft stamps, cutouts, vegetable prints, or crayons. Punch holes in the top and use yarn to make handles.
    2. Wrap with the Sunday comics section. Add a colorful bow.
    3. Wrap with plain white paper. Instead of ribbon, use a man's tie. Perfect for dads or prospective missionaries.
    4. Place gift in a glass or jar and cover top with a bright circle of material. Tie in place with ribbon, yarn, raffia, or embroidered thread.
    5. Wrap in a map. Great way to wrap a going-away gift.
    6. Wrap in a piece of inexpensive, but colorful, fabric.
    7. Use the following ideas instead of ribbon: shoelaces, raffia, measuring tape, strips of old material, or rope.
    8. Embellish packages with pencils, candy canes, silk flowers, cinnamon cutouts (see page 100), or other small items.

- Provide time for sharing ideas and answering possible questions.
- Give every young woman a small box and wrapping paper. Make sure tape and scissors are available.
- Teach the young women how to do a simple wrap on their boxes and allow each young woman to participate in this activity.

Memories of Grandma
Divine Nature, Individual Worth, Knowledge

Gospel Purpose

To help the young women and mothers develop closer relationships.

Activity Description

Each young woman and her mother will share a brief memory of her grandmother and then participate in an evening of "Games that Grandma might have played."

Preparation

1. Discuss the activity in your youth presidency meeting. For youth involvement, select appropriate assignments from this preparation section.
2. Select three or more games listed below for this activity.
3. Have each young woman be prepared to relate something she remembers about her grandmother.*
4. Contact each mother and ask her to be prepared to tell something she remembers about her grandmother.*

Materials Needed: Any materials necessary for chosen games, light refreshments.

Activity

- Gather the young women and their mothers. Briefly talk about how learning about other family members can help draw us closer together. Ask a mother and daughter to share their thoughts about their grandmothers. Give everyone the opportunity to talk about their grandmothers.
- Explain that the games you will be playing were favorites of children when their grandmothers were young.
- Begin game time.

Duck, Duck, Goose—All players sit in a circle, except the player who is "It." She walks around the outside of the circle and touches each other player's head, saying "Duck." After calling out "Duck" a few times, "It" touches a head and says "Goose." The player who is the Goose has to jump up and chase "It" around the circle. If "It" runs around the circle and sits in Goose's spot without being tagged, the Goose becomes "It."

Gunnysack Relay—Have everyone divide into two groups and form two lines. Give the first young woman a gunnysack. She should step inside the sack and hold the sides up. The object of this game is to jump toward the finish line. When she reaches the end of the relay course she should step out of the bag, run back to the starting line and give the sack to the next person. Continue until everyone has had a turn.

Ringtaw—Draw a large circle on the ground and smaller circle inside of it. Place several small marbles, called nibs, in the small circle. From the outside of the large circle, the players take turns flicking a large marble, called a shooter, into the circles. The goal is to knock the nibs out of the circles.

Jackstraws—To play, you must have a pile of wood splinters that are heaped in the middle of a hard surface. Each player has a turn removing one stick from the pile. The challenge is to do so without moving any of the other sticks. A suggestion for Jackstraws might be Pick-up Sticks or skewer sticks.

Ring Toss—Cut stiff rope in twenty-inch lengths. Shape into circles and secure ends with heavy tape. Drive stakes into the ground, leaving about eight to ten inches above ground. Determine the appropriate tossing distance for young women, marking a line for everyone to stand behind as they toss the rings. The objective is for a person to toss the rope ring over the stakes. An indoor variation of this can be done by using cans of soup in place of stakes.

Tiddlywinks—Use chalk or masking tape to draw a circle on a hard surface. Place a cup in the center of that circle. Players use a flat disk, called a shooter, to flip other disks, called winks, into that cup. The object is to be the first player to get all of her winks in the cup. In a timed game, the winner is the player who gets the most winks in the cup before time is up.

Three-legged Race—Mark off a course of about thirty yards. Pair up the mothers and daughters. Tie the daughter's right leg to her mother's left leg. Have the teams race to the finish line. The first one to cross the finish line is declared the winner.

- Encourage the young women and their mothers to write three or more memories about their grandmothers in their journals.
- Enjoy refreshments.

* Be sensitive to individuals who may not have had the opportunity to know their grandmothers. Have them bring something that may have belonged to their grandmothers or relate a story they have heard from someone else.

Communication Skills
Individual Worth, Knowledge

Gospel Purpose

To demonstrate the importance of effective communication.

Activity Description

The young women use several activities to learn about different kinds of communication.

Preparation

1. Discuss the activity in your youth presidency meeting. For youth involvement, select appropriate assignments from this preparation section.
2. If you desire, involve other adults in the setup and communication areas.
3. Select three or more communication activities or use some of your own. Be sensitive to the abilities and needs of your class.

Materials Needed: Check selected communication activities for necessary materials.

Activity

- Briefly discuss what it means to communicate. Have the young women name some of the many ways people communicate.
- Play each selected game or activity and have the young women name the kind of communication they experienced as each one is finished.

Verbal communication 1—Divide the young women into pairs and have them sit back to back. Give Person One a picture with several interconnecting shapes and Person Two a pencil and paper. Using verbal descriptions, Person One must help her partner draw a duplicate of the picture. After a specified length of time, switch roles with a new picture.

Verbal communication 2—Divide the young women into pairs and blindfold one. The blindfolded young woman must use her partner's verbal instruction to accomplish some simple task. Use tasks such as stacking several blocks, putting lids on several different-sized jars, walking through a maze, and so forth.

Foreign language—Have someone speak to the young women in a foreign language. Talk briefly about how communication takes place in every language. Teach one or two simple phrases in a foreign language.

Body language—Write several emotions on individual slips of paper and have each young woman choose one. Act out the chosen emotion without making any sound.

Sign language—Ask someone to talk about how hearing impaired (deaf) individuals "speak" to others. Teach the alphabet and a few simple words or phrases in sign language.

Written communication—Divide the young women into groups of two and give each group several pieces of paper. Tell the young women to find out about the other person (birthdate, favorite color, special experience, and so on) using only written questions and answers. If time permits, have the young women share what they learned about each other.

Written codes—On a chalkboard, write the code translator you will be using. Write a simple coded sentence on pieces of paper. If you desire, use Morse code or another well-known code.

- Briefly discuss communication skills and places the young women will need these skills.

Gospel Purpose

To provide an opportunity for mothers and daughters to work together on a service project.

Activity Description

The young women will organize and, with their mothers, carry out a beautification activity.

Preparation

1. Discuss the activity in your youth presidency meeting. For youth involvement, select appropriate assignments from this preparation section.
2. Contact community leaders to learn about possible projects. Be sure to inquire about funding for materials such as paint, plants, and so forth.
3. Decide on a project. Be sure to plan a project large enough to involve all the mothers and daughters. Make an idea list of specific assignments.
4. After the project is determined, call the appropriate community organization and notify them of your decision.
5. Contact the young women and their mothers about appropriate dress for this activity. Be sensitive to the needs of any young woman who would be without a mother for this activity.
6. Provide for adequate transportation, if necessary. Fill out any necessary travel permits required by your ward or stake.

Materials Needed: Dependent on the service project chosen.

Activity

- Travel to the service activity.
- Distribute any necessary materials or equipment for this activity. Give assignments as necessary.

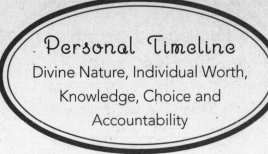

Personal Timeline
Divine Nature, Individual Worth, Knowledge, Choice and Accountability

Gospel Purpose

To help each young woman gain a perspective of what has happened thus far in her life.

Activity Description

Each young woman will make a timeline that features her life.

Preparation

1. Discuss the activity in your youth presidency meeting. For youth involvement, select appropriate assignments from this preparation section.
2. Contact the young women and ask them to bring a list of important dates in their lives.
3. Make your own timeline for the young women to see.

Materials Needed: Paper, pencils, rulers, stickers or markers, plastic sheet protectors.

Activity

- Explain what a timeline is and what it depicts.
- Give each young woman a piece of paper and have her draw a straight line lengthwise.
- Have each young woman write her birthdate at the beginning of the line.
- Show the young women how to enter other important dates on a timeline and have them proceed to do so.
- Decorate the timelines with stickers and markers.
- Place each young woman's timeline into a plastic sheet protector and suggest that the timelines be put into a journal or personal history folder.
- Explain that this is only the beginning of each girl's timeline. Briefly discuss other things that will be placed on their timelines (high school or college graduation, temple marriage, children, and so forth). Help them understand that the choices they make will be part of their mortal timelines.

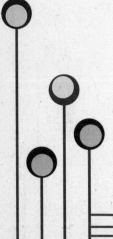

Skills Fair
Knowledge, Good Works

Gospel Purpose

To teach the young women that as they learn and develop skills they will be prepared to help and serve others.

Activity Description

The young women will rotate to three short workshops on child care, CPR, and sign language, or other ideas of your choice.

Preparation

1. Discuss the activity in your youth presidency meeting. For youth involvement, select appropriate assignments from this preparation section.
2. Choose individuals from your ward to teach each workshop. Invite your specialists and give them details such as time considerations, number of girls, and so on. Explain that the purpose of the workshops is to help the young women understand the need for developing particular skills and their benefits to others. Workshops should offer a basic introduction into what is involved in mastering the featured skill and information on how to learn more about it.
3. Assistance as requested by specialists.
4. Prepare a display area with pamphlets that give information of future classes and opportunities to learn the skills being discussed in the workshops.

Materials Needed: Simple refreshments, materials requested by specialists, information pamphlets.

Activity

- Open by introducing the teachers of the workshops. Tell your group that they will be rotating through the different workshops at specific time intervals.
- Participate in the workshops.
- Encourage the young women to view the display table and take pamphlets.
- Serve refreshments.

Follow-up Activity

- As a group, take a CPR class and become certified.

Missionary Letters
Individual Worth, Choice and Accountability, Good Works

Gospel Purpose

To show support for full-time missionaries.

Activity Description

The young women will prepare a group letter for the full-time missionaries serving from their ward/branch.

Preparation

1. Discuss the activity in your youth presidency meeting. For youth involvement, select appropriate assignments from this preparation section.
2. Invite a returned missionary to talk about how it felt to receive mail from ward members. Ask him or her to include ideas about appropriate support. Give your speaker a specific time limit.
3. Cut a sheet of wrapping paper (about 24" x 30") for each missionary. Write the name of one missionary at the top of each sheet of wrapping paper.
4. Contact missionary families and ask for current addresses. If you desire, envelopes can be addressed before the activity begins.
5. Provide plenty of writing room for each paper. Use several tables, the edge of a stage, or the floor.

Materials Needed: Fine-tipped markers, large envelopes, wrapping paper.

Activity

- Have the young women gather to hear the speaker.
- Encourage the young women to write or draw encouraging notes on the back of the wrapping paper. Remind them to individualize each message.
- Continue with the activity until every young woman has had the opportunity to write to every missionary.
- Fold the "letters" up and insert into appropriate envelope.

Service Dinner
Knowledge, Good Works

Gospel Purpose

To experience the joy that accompanies serving others.

Activity Description

As a group, the young women will prepare and deliver dinner to a family in your ward or branch.

Preparation

1. Discuss the activity in your youth presidency meeting. For youth involvement, select appropriate assignments from this preparation section.
2. Contact your Relief Society president to determine a family or individual that may need a meal. Schedule a date and time for the meal to be brought to the family.
3. Plan a simple menu that the young women can prepare.

Materials Needed: Necessary ingredients to prepare your planned menu, supplies for the young women to make a card to deliver with the meal.

Activity

- Discuss the menu with the young women and delegate assignments for meal preparation.
- Prepare the meal and help the girls as needed.
- Assign some of the young women to make a greeting card for the family. Have all the girls sign it.
- Deliver the meal.

**Compassionate
Service Activity**
Individual Worth, Choice and
Accountability, Good Works

Gospel Purpose

To help the young women understand and show compassionate service.

Activity Description

The young women will visit a hospital, nursing home, or an individual that might need compassionate service. Although fresh flowers are always nice, many individuals cannot tolerate the pollen or fragrance. Consider bringing a bouquet of paper flowers ("Paper Flowers," page 81).

Preparation

1. Discuss the activity in your youth presidency meeting. For youth involvement, select appropriate assignments from this preparation section.
2. Before your visit, help the young women determine how they will interact with those that they are visiting. Suggest a song, a short story, a bunch of flowers, specific questions to ask. Help them understand that a sincere interest is the key to a good visit.
3. Provide for adequate transportation, if necessary. Fill out any travel permits required by the ward or stake.

Materials Needed: Determined by the activity.

Activity

- Travel to the predetermined service activity.
- Assist the young women, as necessary, in this activity.

Follow-up Activity

- "Arranging Flowers" on page 24 is an excellent follow-up activity.
- As the plants from your garden flower, make floral arrangements to take to the elderly, those with illnesses, those in nursing homes, or to show appreciation to a leader, and so on.

Personal Protection
Individual Worth, Knowledge, Choice and Accountability

Gospel Purpose

To learn basic personal protection ideas.

Activity Description

The young women will participate in an activity that will assist them in knowing how to practice self-protection.

Preparation

1. Discuss the activity in your youth presidency meeting. For youth involvement, select appropriate assignments from this preparation section.
2. Invite a guest speaker to come and talk about some aspect of self-protection. Be sure to give your specialist all the information (goals, time limits, and financial guidelines) necessary for this activity. Your local police department is an excellent resource.
3. Determine how many of the role-playing situations listed below will be used. Decide if they will be used at the beginning or end of the activity.
4. This is an appropriate activity to invite mothers to attend.

Activity

- Role-play each of the chosen situations. Use any of the following or others of your own creation.

  1. Someone comes to your house and tells you that he is a plumber and needs to fix your plumbing. What should you do? (If you are alone, do not answer the door to strangers. Ask to see identification.)
  2. A phone call is for a parent but you are home alone for the weekend. What should you say? (Indicate that the parent is busy and will return the call. Do not tell the caller that you are alone.)
  3. You answer the phone and someone on the other end begins swearing or using obscene language. What should you say? (Don't say anything. Hang up immediately. If the calls persist, notify the police immediately.)
  4. You are babysitting and the parents come home after dark. You live just around the corner and the parents don't seem to be getting ready to take you home. What should you do? (Ask the mother to take you home or call your parent to come get you.)
  5. Someone you don't know asks you to babysit. What should you say? (Before agreeing to babysit, counsel with your parents. Have them follow up and find out about the family that asked you.)

6. You are returning from a walk and you notice that your house's door looks like it has been damaged. What should you do? (Do not go into the house. Go immediately to a neighbor's house and telephone the police.)

7. Someone you do not know pulls his car up to the curb and asks you for directions. What should you tell him? (Move away from him, and from a safe distance direct him to a local business for directions; but watch carefully for any sign of him leaving his car. If he looks like he will be getting out of the vehicle, do not stay or answer; run to the nearest safe house immediately.)

- Introduce your guest speaker. Assist as necessary.

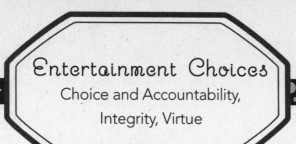

Entertainment Choices
Choice and Accountability,
Integrity, Virtue

Gospel Purpose

To recognize the value of choosing uplifting and wholesome entertainment.

Activity Description

The young women will watch a pre-taped TV show and discuss reasons why it would be considered good entertainment. Letters of appreciation will be written to the television station manager.

Preparation

1. Discuss the activity in your youth presidency meeting. For youth involvement, select appropriate assignments from this preparation section.
2. Prayerfully select an appropriate TV show for the young women to view. Record the show in advance.
3. Obtain the name and address of the television station that aired the show.

Materials Needed: DVD player, television, DVD, paper, envelopes, pens.

Activity

- Show the DVD.
- Read Article of Faith 13. Discuss why the show was appropriate. Point out that we must be very selective in the things we choose for entertainment.
- Instruct each young woman to write a letter of appreciation to the television station manager. Assist them as needed.
- Address and mail letters.

Cinnamon Cutouts
Knowledge, Good Works

Gospel Purpose

To give the young women an opportunity for socializing, friendshipping, and building feelings of self-worth.

Activity Description

The young women will make cinnamon fragrance cutouts to give as gifts or for part of an activity such as "Gift Wrap Ideas" (page 86) or "Christmas Tree Decorating" (page 71).

Preparation

1. Discuss the activity in your youth presidency meeting. For youth involvement, select appropriate assignments from this preparation section.
2. Have each young woman bring a 75 milliliter can of cinnamon, rolling pins, and any small Christmas cookie cutters.
3. Make the craft yourself and review any potential problems for possible solutions.

Materials Needed: Thin ribbon, pencils, flour, applesauce, waxed paper, cookie sheets or large, flat boards.

Activity

- Combine 1/3 cup flour and 1/3 cup cinnamon (75 ml can) in a bowl.
- Add 2/3 cup applesauce and mix until completely blended. Dough will be very stiff.
- Place dough on a cutting board and roll out until it is 1/4 inch thick.
- Cut out shapes with cookie cutter. This recipe will make about twelve shapes.
- Use a pencil to gently make a hole in the top of each shape.
- Line a cookie sheet with waxed paper.
- Place shapes on waxed paper and allow to dry for two to three days.
- Thread ribbon through the holes of each shape and tie the tops with an overhand or square knot.
- Give shapes as a gift, hang them where they will fill the air with fragrance, or use them to decorate a Christmas tree.